San Diego Guide to Military Ships and Planes

W9-BEX-327

by J. Halpern

PS Features
San Diego

For additional copies of this book, visit your local bookstore or contact the publisher. See the coupon on page 94.

For groups and organizations, a discount price is available.

Copyright @ 1989
PS Features

Printed in the United States of America

Published by PS Features
P. O. Box 6751
San Diego, California 92106-6751

Production by K-W Publishing Services, San Diego, CA 92126

ISBN 0-9622926-0-5

Library of Congress 89-091057

First Printing

10 9 8 7 6 5 4 3 2 1

to Opal Howard Cokely,
a woman whose commitment to the military family
has been long-lived and sincere

Table of Contents

Acknowledgments

When a civilian sets out to write a book about the U.S. Navy and Marine Corps, there is no end to the list of persons she must thank for help. There are so many ways to make mistakes that it is essential to have knowledgeable persons walk a writer through the information.

The man who opened the door to that information was LtGen. Joseph C. Fegan, USMC (Ret.), a good neighbor, a fine Marine, and a great man. Capt. John L. Vandegrift, USMC (Ret.), has so much first-hand knowledge from his experience as a fighter pilot that he is a superb teacher in his role as Deputy of Public Affairs, Commander Naval Base San Diego. He has an eye for detail, a great sense of humor, and a passion for excellence that makes a writer reach for the best way to say things. VADM Nels Johnson, USN (Ret.), who recently passed away, was a tremendous help in providing materials for study. Thomas P. Faulconer has the gift of making airplane design understandable to the lay person. To these men, my thanks for sharing knowledge and resources.

RADM J. B. Finkelstein, Navy Chief of Information in Washington, D.C., permitted me access to a very busy staff of public affairs officers assigned to the various military bases in San Diego. These persons are among the best communicators in the business. In spite of a heavy workload, they took time to explain the smallest details about the mission and methods of their bases.

The public affairs officers whose help was essential to this book include: CDR David Dillon, USN; LCDR Bob Pritchard, USN; LT Ken Luchka, USN; LT Michael Dillon, USN; LT Sonja Hedley, USN; GySgt. Larry Crutchfield, USMC; SSgt. John Midgette, USMC; JOC Bobbie Carleton, USN; JO2 Chiquita Land, USN; Mrs. Julie Swan, and Mr. Ken Mitchell.

Joni Halpern

Foreword

For a newcomer to the San Diego area, the Navy presence can be awesome. From the Embaradero, there seems to be a constant going and returning of ships . . . "haze, grey, and underway."

Across the channel at North Island, one can almost always see the huge bulk of one or more of the three carriers homeported here, augmented, on occasion, by one of the even more massive nuclear-powered carriers visiting from up north.

Helicopters of various makes, models, and missions swirl up from North Island. Transports and anti-submarine aircraft take off and land on the air station's runways, interspersed with fighters and attack aircraft on test flights after renovation at North Island Depot. And all this constitutes but a small slice of Navy and Marine Corps activity in the San Diego area. To say that it is impressive, spectacular, even dazzling to the uninitiated and uninformed is an understatement on the order of saying Pavarotti can sing a little.

There has long been a need for a book to explain to the visitor, of if you will, the tourist, what goes on here in easily understood, non-technical language, beginning with the basics. For example, I think it is a good thing for the average man-on-the-street to know the difference between a "ship" and a "boat." (A boat is a small craft capable of being hoisted aboard a ship. Submarines are perhaps the only exception; submariners still refer to their underwater monsters as "boats.") And to be aware that only a few of the Navy's combatants are battleships. ("Hey, Daddy, look at all those battleships out there" . . . "Wrong, son.")

Mrs. Halpern's book describes the many different classes of ships that the Navy has here in the area and some others that are frequent visitors. Her descriptions are accurate and succinct, and the accompanying photographs make identification easy for even the most inexperienced layman. She does an equally excellent job with regard to Navy aircraft. Words and photos make I.D. easy.

In brief, this book fills the aforementioned need and fills it well. It has been painstakingly researched. It is factual and eminently readable. Beyond that, it contains a number of cogent editorial comments augmenting the text that the reader will find well worth "the price of admission."

In its coverage of the spectrum of naval weaponry, Mrs. Halpern's book does credit to the men and women without whom it would all be so much useless cold metal, the men and women who make it all come together, the men and women who give us the edge.

Finally, it is probably well worth the reader's effort to keep in mind as he or she looks around San Diego and bears witness to this incredible panoply of military power, and the staggering total of tax dollars it represents, that this is the one sword that keeps the other in its sheath.

> **Capt. John L. Vandegrift, USMC, (Ret.)**
> **Deputy of Public Affairs**
> **Commander Naval Base San Diego**

Introduction

This guide was written with two things in mind. First, it is intended to be a quick reference for the tourist in our area who wants the answers to a few simple questions. What kinds of Navy ships am I seeing in the harbor? What are those aircraft flying overhead? Where can I go to see a U.S. Navy or Marine Corps recruit graduation? Can I visit a submarine? What happens at Camp Pendleton? This reference book will answer those questions and more.

The second goal of this book is to open the tourist's eyes to an incredible exhibit of American military preparedness. If you've ever wondered what the military does with its budget, San Diego is one of the best exhibits of the kind of power this budget buys. San Diego is said to be the largest naval complex in the free world. More than 100 ships and nearly 150,000 active-duty Navy and Marine Corps personnel call this county home. The Navy says those figures comprise about one-sixth of its total combatant fleet. Many of the major components of that fleet are shown in this guide.

For reasons of safety, efficiency, and security, a great deal of military activity is closed to the public. Even so, in San Diego, there is plenty for a visitor to see and experience. The Navy and Marine Corps welcome those who want a closer look at our fighting forces. Using this guide will make it easier to do so.

Map Key and Directions

1 **Broadway Pier**
   The pier is an extension of Broadway, which intersects Harbor Drive along the Embarcadero. Broadway is downtown San Diego's main street.

2 **Camp Pendleton**
   From San Diego, take I-5 North 38 miles to Oceanside, exiting at the Camp Pendleton/Harbor Drive off-ramp. Stop at the Main Gate.

3 **MCRD**
   Take I-5 South (just past the Sea World Drive exit) to the Rosecrans turnoff. I-8 West also has a Rosecrans exit. Go left on Lytton St. Follow Lytton as it becomes Barnett. Stay in right lane as Barnett breaks into Pacific Highway. Exit at Witherby to gate.

4 **NAS Miramar**
   Take I-15 North to Miramar Way exit. Turn left, cross bridge over freeway, and proceed to Main Gate.

5 **NAS North Island**
   Take I-5 South to Coronado Bridge exit. Cross bridge, and proceed along 4th St. to end, where signs will direct you to Main Gate.

6 **Naval Sub Base (Ballast Point)**
   Follow Rosecrans (accessible from I-5 South or I-8 West) until you reach the Main Gate. Directions to the base may be obtained from the guard.

7 **Naval Station San Diego (Foot of 32nd Street)**
   From San Diego, take I-5 South to 28th St. Turn right. Make a left on Main Street and proceed to Gate.

8 **Naval Training Center**
   Take I-5 South (just past the Sea World Drive exit) to the Rosecrans turnoff. I-8 West also has a Rosecrans exit. Go left on Lytton St., and enter first gate. Additional gate, past Lytton on Rosecrans.

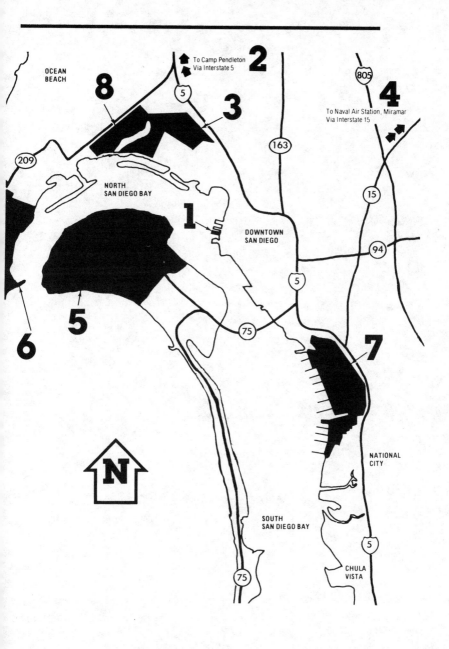

OCEAN BEACH

8

2
To Camp Pendleton
Via Interstate 5

3

805

4

To Naval Air Station, Miramar
Via Interstate 15

209

163

15

NORTH
SAN DIEGO BAY

1

DOWNTOWN
SAN DIEGO

94

5

5

6

75

7

NATIONAL
CITY

N

SOUTH
SAN DIEGO BAY

5

CHULA
VISTA

75

Ships

Identifying naval ships takes a little practice, but it can be fun. We have provided a number of tools to make the job easier.

Use the ship silhouettes on the following pages to help you identify some of the most common types of Navy ships seen in San Diego. If you can't find a ship silhouette that matches the ship you've spotted in the harbor, flip through the pictures that accompany the written descriptions of each type of ship. It was not possible to list every Navy ship in San Diego, but most of them are included in this guide.

We have included a summary of each ship to tell you about its general design, its mission, and its armaments. You may be able to supplement this knowledge with a first-hand tour of a ship.

Weekly Tour of Ships

Almost every Saturday and Sunday, 1 p.m. to 4 p.m., at least one Navy ship docks at the Broadway Pier along the Embarcadero to allow the public a chance to tour it. Call 235-3534 for details.

Quick Reference Guide to Military Ships in Local Waters

These are just a few of the most common types. See the following pages for a full description of all the major ships in the San Diego area.

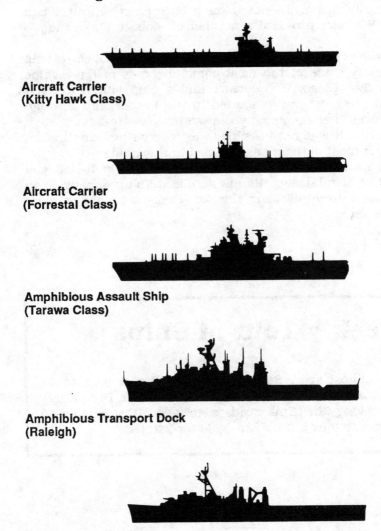

**Aircraft Carrier
(Kitty Hawk Class)**

**Aircraft Carrier
(Forrestal Class)**

**Amphibious Assault Ship
(Tarawa Class)**

**Amphibious Transport Dock
(Raleigh)**

**Amphibious Transport Dock
(Austin Class)**

**AEGIS Cruiser
(Ticonderoga Class)**

**Destroyer
(Spruance Class)**

**Dock Landing Ship
(Thomaston Class)**

**Dock Landing Ship
(Anchorage Class)**

**Frigate
(Knox Class)**

**Frigate
(Oliver Hazard Perry Class)**

Ship Letters Guide

AALC	amphibious assault landing craft
AD	destroyer tender
AE	ammunition ship
AFS	combat stores ship
AG	miscellaneous
AGF	miscellaneous command ship
AGS	surveying ship
AO	oiler
AOE	fast combat support ship
AOR	replenishment oiler
AR	repair ship
ARL	repair ship, small
ARS	salvage ship
AS	submarine tender
ASR	submarine rescue ship
ATF	fleet tug
ATS	salvage and rescue ship
BB	battleship
CG	guided-missile cruiser
CGN	nuclear-powered guided-missile cruiser
CV	aircraft carrier
CVN	nuclear-powered aircraft carrier
DD	destroyer
DDG	guided-missile destroyer
DSRV	deep-submergence rescue vehicle
DSV	deep-submergence vehicle
FF	frigate
FFG	guided-missile frigate
LCAC	landing craft air-cushion
LCC	amphibious command ship
LCM	mechanized landing craft
LCU	utility landing craft
LCVP	landing craft vehicle and personnel
LHA	amphibious assault ship
LKA	amphibious cargo ship
LPD	amphibious transport dock
LPH	amphibious assault ship
LSD	dock landing ship
LST	tank landing ship

Aircraft Carriers

USS Constellation, CV-64, aircraft carrier (photo courtesy of U.S. Navy)

The aircraft carrier was conceived after World War I for the purpose of protecting and defending a battle fleet that had at its center the massive battleship. Today, it is abundantly clear that the aircraft carrier is an offensive weapon unto itself, with an ability to attack any target, whether on land or sea.

By far the largest ship in the American Navy, the modern carrier is more than 1,000 feet long, with a flight deck about 250 feet wide. Its four propeller shafts are powered by either nuclear or conventional fuel engines. There are no nuclear-powered carriers home-based in San Diego. Carriers here have a main propulsion plant that is about 280 feet long and 90 feet wide. Four turbines produce a total horsepower of 280,000 under full power. To run this powerhouse, the ship carries about 2.6 million gallons of fuel oil.

Eighty to 90 aircraft are assigned to each carrier, including, among others, the famous F-14 Tomcat, F/A-18 Hornet, S-3 Viking, ASW aircraft, helicopters, and the easily recognized E-2C Hawkeye. Jets are launched from the flight deck by means of four steam catapults which hurl the planes into the air at varying speeds, depending upon the speed of the wind and the ship, as well as the weight of the plane. An F-14 with a full payload would be launched by the catapult at about 150 knots.

The launch, flight, and recovery of aircraft are heavily

dependent upon mechanical and computer systems operated by a staff whose fluidity and timing are unsurpassed by any carrier crews in the world. A carrier has a ship's company of about 3,000 persons and an aircrew of over 2,000.

An aircraft carrier never travels alone, even though it carries missiles, guns, and planes for its own protection. Instead, the carrier becomes the centerpiece in a battle group in which cruisers, destroyers, and frigates surround it, using their sophisticated weapons and tracking systems to screen the carrier from harm.

Even from afar, the aircraft carrier is one of the most compelling sights in San Diego Harbor. It is easy to understand why an Air Force officer visiting on bridge of a carrier said, "It's like steering Central Park from the Empire State Building." (from Hanson W. Baldwin's book, THE NEW NAVY)

Aircraft carriers assigned to San Diego dock at North Island. They can be seen from various points along the waterfront, including Seaport Village, the Embarcadero, Harbor Island, and Shelter Island. To inquire about whether you may visit a carrier, follow the instructions in the Facilities Section of this book on Page 78.

Aircraft carriers in San Diego include:

USS Ranger	CV-61
USS Independence	CV-62
USS Constellation	CV-64

Amphibious Assault Ships

USS Tarawa, LHA-1, amphibious assault ship

Amphibious assault ships look like small aircraft carriers, and in a sense, they are. They carry 11 to 26 helicopters and four to eight Harrier jets. They also carry a Marine battalion landing team and its equipment, plus the landing vehicles necessary to transport them to shore. The amphibious assault ship is probably the most sophisticated means by which men and equipment are transported for an assault against a defended shore.

The oldest of the amphibious assault ships, the Iwo Jima Class, was the world's first ship with a flight deck designed specifically to operate helicopters. It has no arresting wires or catapults. Two elevator platforms operate off the deck edge, one to port, the other to starboard.

The Tarawa Class at 820 feet is about 200 feet longer than the Iwo Jima Class. Like the latter, however, the Tarawa Class amphibious assault ships can carry almost 2,000 Marines and their equipment. In the ships of the Tarawa class, landing craft are launched by means of a floodable docking well. Water is allowed to enter the docking well to a level sufficient to float the landing craft. When the craft are released, the water is pumped out.

Tarawa Class ships have two hangars beneath the flight deck, and like the ships of the Iwo Jima Class, they have extensive medical facilities, including diagnostic imaging and operating rooms, laboratories, and a pharmacy.

The Wasp Class is the newest line of amphibious assault ships and will enter service soon. The general configuration of these ships is much the same as in earlier classes, but with marked improvements in load management and capability, construction of the island (which contains the bridge), and expansion of hospital facilities.

Amphibious assault ships in San Diego include:

USS Tarawa	LHA-1
USS Belleau Wood	LHA-3
USS Okinawa	LPH-3
USS Tripoli	LPH-10
USS New Orleans	LPH-11

Amphibious Cargo Ships

USS Durham, LKA-114, amphibious cargo ship

Amphibious cargo ships are designed to carry heavy equipment, supplies, and men for assaults on enemy shores. They are operated by 350 persons and carry about 360 Marine troops and up to nine mechanized landing craft (LCM).

Each cargo ship has two cranes that can lift almost 80 tons each, two booms with a 40-ton capacity each, and eight booms with 15-ton capacity each. The amphibious cargo ship is more easily identified if you remember the superstructure is amidship, with booms and cranes fore and aft.

An amphibious cargo ship in San Diego is:

USS Durham   LKA-114

Amphibious Transport Docks

USS Vancouver, LPD-2, amphibious transport dock

Amphibious transport docks are ships that carry Marines, their equipment, and supplies to coastal landing areas. Troops disembark by means of helicopters, landing craft, or amphibious vehicles that are launched from the docking well at the stern. Ramps allow vehicles to be driven from the permanent helicopter flight deck to the garages or docking well below.

The ship can be identified by the tiered superstructure set forward, with a boom crane amidship, and the helicopter platform covering the entire docking well. At the stern is a door that becomes a ramp when opened onto the water.

Amphibious transport docks carry about 930 Marines, a ship's company of more than 400, and four to nine mechanized landing craft (LCM). Up to six of the big Sea Knight helicopters (the ones with two rotors) also can be carried.

Amphibious transport docks in San Diego include:

USS Vancouver	LPD-2
USS Denver	LPD-9
USS Juneau	LPD-10

Attack Submarines

USS Sturgeon, SSN-637, attack submarine

The mission of the attack submarine is to find and destroy enemy submarines and ships before they can be used against the United States or its allies. Attack submarines are part of a forward force that, in the event of war, would try to incapacitate the enemy's ability to attack us from the sea.

To accomplish this, the attack submarine is designed to be as silent and swift as is technologically possible. It carries the most advanced tracking systems, missiles, and torpedoes, and its crews are among the best-trained in the world. It is nuclear-powered and can stay submerged for extended periods. The life of the reactor core itself is estimated at 10 years.

To counter the increasing capabilities of enemy submarines, the U.S. Navy is developing a new class of attack submarine called Seawolf (SSN-21). This class will be quieter, faster, and more sensitive in tracking and responding to an enemy threat. The challenge in designing the Seawolf has been to match and even exceed the capabilities of the most advanced Soviet design, and yet, to leave room for improvements in power and technology that will keep Seawolf competitive into the 21st Century.

Submarines based in San Diego and elsewhere are not open to the general public. But sometimes tour groups are permitted aboard, with strict limitations on viewing, provided the guidelines listed in the Facilities Section on Page 84 are met.

Attack submarines in San Diego include:

USS Permit	SSN-594
USS Plunger	SSN-595
USS Barb	SSN-596
USS Pollack	SSN-603
USS Haddo	SSN-604
USS Jack	SSN-605
USS Guardfish	SSN-612
USS Flasher	SSN-613
USS Pogy	SSN-647
USS Puffer	SSN-652
USS Guitarro	SSN-665
USS Pintado	SSN-672
USS Drum	SSN-677
USS Wm. H. Bates	SSN-680
USS La Jolla	SSN-701
USS Portsmouth	SSN-707
USS Salt Lake City	SSN-716

Ballistic Missile Submarines

USS Ohio, SSBN-726, ballistic missile submarine

There are no ballistic missile submarines homeported in San Diego. Yet, as a category, even though they are rarely seen here, they should be mentioned briefly, because they comprise a full 50 per cent of the United States nuclear deterrent. Ballistic missiles are designed to run fast, silent, and deep, so they will stand the least possible chance of being detected by the enemy prior to their launching of missiles.

These submarines carry as many as 24 ballistic missiles, each of which has several independently targetable warheads. Ballistic missile submarines also carry weapons for their own defense.

Every class of SSBN built prior to the Ohio Class is about 20 years old and will be replaced by the powerful, modern Trident nuclear submarine. All SSBNs in the American Navy are nuclear-powered, enabling them to remain at sea for as long as their crews can hold out. During peacetime, the usual patrol for a single crew is 70 days.

The Ohio Class SSBNs are 560 feet long, 42 feet wide, and 35.5 feet deep. They carry 24 Trident missiles, each with six to eight separately targeted warheads that can strike land targets thousands of miles away.

Battleships

USS New Jersey, BB-62, battleship

There was a time not long ago when the battleship reigned supreme on the ocean. Nothing could compare to her powerful guns, thick skin, and great endurance. But the development of the modern aircraft carrier, with the breadth and range of its capabilities, supplanted the battleship, leaving the United States, for a period in the recent past, without a single operating battleship. During that time, it became clear that the loss of the battleship hurt the overall flexibility of American naval defenses.

So it was that Congress in 1981 funded the modernization and recommissioning of four World War II battleships. At this writing, all four ships — Iowa, New Jersey, Missouri, and Wisconsin — have been reactivated. These ships are an impressive 887 feet long, with sleek hulls, and banks of massive guns. They have nine 16-inch guns, 12 five-inch guns, a main belt of armor 12 inches thick, and a crew of about 1,800 officers and men.

As part of its modernization, today's battleship is fitted with the most advanced electronic warfare systems, missiles, communication, and radar systems, along with helicopter platforms. Crew quarters, galleys, and other areas have been updated.

But the characteristics that still set the battleship apart, in addition to its size, are the firepower from its huge guns and the thickness of its skin. For example, its 16-inch guns have giant rifled barrels that fire a 1,000-pound shell a distance of about 30 miles with near-pinpoint accuracy. When all of the battleship's firepower is considered, no other ship, with the exception of the aircraft carrier, can deliver such a devastating offensive blow. And, the battleship's heavy hull allows it to survive certain kinds of counterstrikes that would sink a lesser ship.

The battleships of the Pacific Fleet — New Jersey and Missouri — are homeported in Long Beach. They are mentioned in this book only because many visitors are hopeful of seeing them during the ships' infrequent visits to San Diego.

Cruisers

USS Vincennes, CG-49, AEGIS guided-missile cruiser

The cruiser used to be a smaller version of the battleship. Today, however, its technological capabilities and armaments have taken it well beyond its mission in earlier wars. The cruiser is now a specialist, capable of tracking and eliminating enemy threats on the surface, in the air, or in the ocean.

It would not be correct to depict the cruiser as a nearly invincible lone wolf, scanning the air, surface, and undersea spaces and disposing miraculously of its enemies. Rather, it is a complex ship that, in spite of its considerable ability to defend itself, works best as part of a network of naval defenses.

The cruiser has gained a new importance in the American Navy because of the installation of the AEGIS missile tracking and guidance system, the most advanced in use today. Using cutting-edge technology, the AEGIS oversees the detection, tracking, and elimination of more than 100 targets at a time in a battle zone. The altitude and speed of a target, whether very high or very low, are of no consequence to the AEGIS; it can detect, track, and kill an extremely wide range of attackers. The presence of this system on the Ticonderoga Class of cruisers has been a significant advantage to American battle groups.

Some cruisers are powered by nuclear reactors, others by conventional fuels. Most cruisers can achieve a speed of about

30 knots or better; at 20 knots, their range is about 6,000 to 8,000 miles.

To the untrained eye, cruisers can be hard to distinguish from destroyers and frigates. The cruiser's hull is 100 to 120 feet longer than that of a frigate. The cruiser's two radar masts are built right onto its funnels. But the differences between a cruiser and a destroyer are best seen by comparing their photos. To be certain as to what you're seeing, however, check the ship's number against those listed here. Also, see if the ship's profile conforms generally to the photograph shown here.

Cruisers in San Diego include:

USS Long Beach	CGN-9
("N" stands for nuclear.)	
USS Leahy	CG-16
USS Gridley	CG-21
USS England	CG-22
USS Halsey	CG-23
USS Jouett	CG-29
USS Horne	CG-30
USS Wm. H. Standley	CG-32
USS Fox	CG-33
USS Truxtun	CGN-35
USS Vincennes	CG-49
USS Valley Forge	CG-50
USS Lake Champlain	CG-57

Destroyers

USS Spruance, DD-963, destroyer

USS Arleigh Burke, DDG-51, guided-missile destroyer

The destroyer is a sleek, fast warship with powerful armaments, detection, and tracking devices designed to hunt and kill submarines and to eliminate enemy threats on the sea or in the air. Destroyers comprise part of the protective screen that operates around a carrier or battleship, but they also accompany replenishment and amphibious groups.

During World War I and the beginning of World War II, the destroyer's job was to knock out hostile ships by using torpedoes. Today, the destroyer is equipped with a variety of weapons to use against a variety of threats. Looking at the surface of a typical Kidd Class destroyer, you can see something of its armaments. Starting at the bow is a five-inch gun that shoots 20 70-pound shells per minute a distance of 12.6 nautical miles. Just behind that gun are two anti-submarine missile launchers. At the top front of the superstructure is a six-barrelled Vulcan Phalanx gun that fires 3,000 heavy-density rounds per minute to a distance of 1.5 kilometers. Amidship, there are two Harpoon missile launchers, each resembling four logs tied together.

The destroyer also has two sets of torpedo launch tubes that fire anti-submarine torpedoes with warheads that weigh almost 100 pounds apiece and travel through the water at 40 knots to a distance of six nautical miles. Repeated on the fantail of the ship are another Phalanx gun and the anti-submarine missile launchers. From bow to stern, the destroyer carries a deadly array of weapons indeed.

The Navy plans 20 new destroyers of the Arleigh Burke Class to come on line during the next few years. These destroyers will have improved survivability, due to all-steel hulls and armor in vital areas. They will carry the AEGIS Combat System previously found only on cruisers.

Destroyers in San Diego include:

USS Henry B. Wilson	DDG-7
USS Lynde McCormick	DDG-8
USS Robison	DDG-12
USS Hoel	DDG-13
USS Berkeley	DDG-15
USS Waddell	DDG-24
USS Kincaid	DDG-965
USS Hewitt	DD-966
USS Elliott	DD-967
USS John Young	DD-973
USS O'Brien	DD-975
USS Merrill	DD-976
USS Ingersoll	DD-990
USS Fletcher	DD-992
USS Callaghan	DDG-994
USS Chandler	DDG-996

Destroyer Tenders

USS Acadia, AD-42, destroyer tender

Destroyer tenders homeported in San Diego were built here by National Steel and Shipbuilding Co. These ships are members of the post-World War II Samuel Gompers Class, for which there was about a 12-year lag between the first three ships and those that followed. Destroyer tenders here are of the more recent group commissioned in the 1980s.

These ships are like floating ship-building companies. They have foundries and furnaces, repair shops, and storage facilities. They also have some crack craftsmen aboard. When the frigate USS Stark was hit by two Exocet missiles in May, 1987, in the Persian Gulf, she sustained massive damage. The destroyer tender USS Acadia had her seaworthy in 30 days.

Destroyer tenders service a variety of ships, including the highly complex guided-missile cruisers. Tenders can service simultaneously six guided-missile destroyers moored alongside.

Destroyer tenders in San Diego include:

USS Acadia	AD-42
USS Cape Cod	AD-43

Dock Landing Ships

USS Alamo, LSD-33, dock landing ship

USS Whidbey Island, LSD-41, dock landing ship

Dock landing ships (LSD) can be mistaken for amphibious transport docks (LPD), which look extremely similar with the superstructure forward, cranes amidship, and helicopter deck aft. The reason for this similarity is that amphibious transport docks were built to replace the older dock landing ships. Therefore, their missions are the same: to transport Marines, their equipment, and landing craft for an assault on a hostile shore.

Except for the new Whidbey Island Class, dock landing ships have a superstructure tiered back from the bow. One funnel is set abaft the superstructure, another amidship, with cranes set abaft the first or second funnel. To this point, they are similar to their kin, the amphibious transport dock, although the latter have a superstructure that looks as if it is molded right out of the hull.

The older dock landing ships have a helicopter platform that does not extend fully to the fantail of the ship, leaving the docking well somewhat open. The amphibious transport dock, on the other hand, has a helicopter platform that is a permanent and complete roof over the docking well. Older dock landing ships can carry about 350 Marines and their equipment, plus about six landing craft.

The newer ships of the Whidbey Island Class, with a super-structure that looks like a large box with a small box in front, can carry about 450 Marines, and a variety of landing craft, including the new air-cushioned type (LCAC). These ships also provide some repair services for landing craft.

An interesting note is that the first ship in the Whidbey Island Class cost $411 million, while the last one will cost only about $220 million. First-time production costs for a new class of ships can be high, especially if production preparations are extensive.

Dock landing ships in San Diego include:

USS Alamo	LSD-33
USS Monticello	LSD-35
USS Fort Fisher	LSD-40
USS Germantown	LSD-42

Frigates

USS Knox, FF-1052, frigate

USS Oliver Hazard Perry, FFG-7, guided-missile frigate

The frigate is smaller than a destroyer in both length and beam. It also has less firepower, although it does carry guns, missiles, and torpedoes for defense against submarines, aircraft, and other ships. The frigate works primarily as an escort with amphibious task groups, underway replenishment groups, or convoys. It is slower than either a destroyer or cruiser, but it can carry guided missiles just as they can.

The frigate can operate two Light Airborne Multi-Purpose System (LAMPS) helicopters from the landing pad on its stern. These helicopters greatly increase the ship's ability to detect enemy threats, because they extend by many miles the detection range. They can tow sonar equipment in the water, and simply by the fact that they can rise to a ceiling of 15,000 feet, helicopters extend the radar range protecting the frigate and the ships she is escorting.

Today's frigates are designed to streamline manpower requirements, and for good reason. Since the beginning of the all-volunteer services in the United States, the Navy always has been able to meet its enlistment quotas. But in recent years, the pool of eligible enlistees has dropped off, and this is of some concern to the Navy. In the most efficient circumstances, it is still a labor-intensive task to operate a 600-ship Navy. Thus, newer ships reflect an effort to conserve manpower.

The newest frigates, the Oliver Hazard Perry Class, are examples of this reduction in manpower needs. The older Knox Class frigates require a ratio of enlisted persons to officers of 18:1. The 50 ships of the Perry Class require a ratio of only 15:1. This class represents other improvements as well, including the fact that its building program is considered the best-managed in the Navy's history. Every Perry Class frigate delivered thus far has been on or ahead of schedule and below cost.

Once again, to the lay person, it may seem hard to distinguish a frigate from a destroyer or cruiser, especially if the frigate is seen singly, without the benefit of size comparisons. But generally, the frigate has one tall radar mast that extends either from the funnel itself or is built amidship with the funnel behind it barely protruding from the superstructure. Ordinarily, the frigate is about 100 feet shorter than a destroyer and about 120 feet shorter than a cruiser. Frigates are more numerous than any other type of combat ship in the Navy.

Frigates in San Diego include:

USS Brooke	FFG-1
USS Ramsey	FFG-2
USS Schofield	FFG-3
USS John A. Moore	FFG-19
USS Lewis B. Puller	FFG-23
USS Copeland	FFG-25

USS Mahlon S. Tisdale	FFG-27
USS Reid	FFG-30
USS McCluskey	FFG-41
USS Thach	FFG-43
USS Rentz	FFG-46
USS Bronstein	FF-1037
USS Bradley	FF-1041
USS Albert David	FF-1050
USS O'Callahan	FF-1051
USS Roark	FF-1053
USS Hepburn	FF-1055
USS Meyerkord	FF-1058
USS Reasoner	FF-1063
USS Stein	FF-1065
USS Marvin Shields	FF-1066
USS Bagley	FF-1069
USS Downes	FF-1070
USS Fanning	FF-1076
USS Cook	FF-1083
USS Barbey	FF-1088

Hospital Ships

USNS Mercy, T-AH-19, hospital ship
(photo reprinted with permission of Union-Tribune Publishing Company)

Occasionally, the giant white hospital ship USNS Mercy (T-AH-19), homeported in Oakland, California, visits San Diego. When it was last here, it tied up at Navy Pier at the foot of Broadway.

USNS Mercy is one of two hospital ships that are part of the United States Military Sealift Command. This command, comprised of over 100 ships operated primarily by civilian crews under the Navy's authority, provides transport services for all branches of the U.S. Military.

USNS Mercy has 1,000 beds, 12 operating rooms, plus diagnostic, therapeutic, and other technical facilities. It has a civilian crew of 68, but its medical, support, and communications personnel are from the Navy. The ship can achieve full operating status within five days of receiving sailing orders.

Submarine Rescue Ships

USS Pigeon, ASR-21, submarine rescue ship

Older submarine rescue ships are adapted from tug boat designs, but the newest ones, the two ships of the Pigeon Class, are designed specifically for their mission of supporting the rescue of men from deeply submerged submarines.

One member of this class of ship is homeported on the Atlantic Coast; the other, USS Pigeon itself, is based here in San Diego. With the exception of one Military Sealift Command ship, USS Pigeon is the first catamaran hull to be built for the Navy since Robert Fulton's steam gunboat of 1812.

Each of the hulls is 251 feet long and 26 feet wide. The distance between the hulls is 34 feet, allowing the servicing, raising, and lowering of two Deep-Submergence Rescue Vehicles. These vehicles look like 50-foot submarines with a shrouded propeller on one end and a half-sphere protruding from their underside. With their precise maneuvering and hovering capabilities, these craft can seal their half-sphere to the hatch of a disabled submarine, locking out the water and enabling men to be transferred from the submarine to the rescue vehicle. Twenty-four persons at a time can be rescued. Deep-Submergence Rescue Vehicles can dive to 5,000 feet.

The submarine rescue ship also supports conventional and saturation diving operations to a depth of 850 feet. It can lower divers to the ocean floor in pressurized transfer chambers for open-sea work. The ship also can serve as the operational control ship for salvage operations.

A submarine rescue ship in San Diego is:

USS Pigeon   ASR-21

29

Submarine Tenders

USS Dixon, AS-37, submarine tender

Submarine tenders homeported in San Diego service, repair, and supply nuclear attack submarines, including those of the Los Angeles Class, which is comprised of some of the Navy's most recently built subs with the most advanced capability to date.

It can be difficult for the lay person to distinguish between the submarine tenders and destroyer tenders homebased in San Diego, especially since they have a similar hull design and profile. There are some differences in the cranes, but these are apparent only if you study the photos carefully. The simplest distinction is the ship's number, visible near the bow. If the number is preceded by an "S," the ship is a submarine tender; if preceded by a "D," the ship is a destroyer tender.

Submarine tenders carry about 600 persons, many of whom are repairmen and technicians. There is also a 23-bed sickbay. Four submarines moored alongside the ship can be serviced simultaneously.

Submarine tenders in San Diego include:

USS Dixon	AS-37
USS McKee	AS-41

Tank Landing Ships

USS Barbour County, LST-1195, tank landing ship

The letters LST belong to a group of ships that probably are the easiest to identify, because of the twin derrick arms that extend from their bow. The arms support a 112-foot ramp that is lowered to offload the tanks. This elevated ramp eliminates the flat bow door which was used as a ramp and prevailed in designs of LSTs during World War II. The change in design, as well as improvements in power, allow modern LSTs to make up to 20 knots.

The massive bow door on present-day LSTs, opened when the ramp must be lowered, operates at the touch of a button, releasing the worm drive that attaches the door to the ship. The stern gate also can be opened to allow amphibious vehicles to be launched directly from the ship.

An LST carries about 250 Marines, their infantry equipment, tanks, and anti-tank vehicles and weapons. Usually this group would be used in a surprise attack on an enemy shore. The infantry goes first, followed by the armored vehicles.

The LST defends itself by means of two rather old guns, each operated by seven men. However, this class of ships will be fitted with six-barrelled, rapid-fire Vulcan Phalanx guns, as well as Stinger missiles.

Tank landing ships in San Diego include:

USS Fresno	LST-1182
USS Peoria	LST-1183
USS Frederick	LST-1184

USS Schenectady	LST-1185
USS Cayuga	LST-1186
USS Tuscaloosa	LST-1187
USS Saginaw	LST-1188
USS San Bernardino	LST-1189
USS Barbour County	LST-1195
USS Bristol County	LST-1198

Other Navy Ships

There are several other types of ships in addition to those mentioned here. There are ships for replenishment of fuel and ammunition, oceanographic research, aviation and logistics support, fast combat support, combat stores, repair, salvage, patrol, command, and a host of other functions. We have included photos and brief descriptions of some of these ships that can be seen in San Diego Harbor.

The American commitment has been to a 600-ship Navy with full combat capabilities on any ocean in the world. Recent developments in the national budget-cutting process may affect the size of the fleet. However, the goals remain the same. Even though the United States is a full continent wide, it functions, in essence, as an island nation. Its commercial, military, and political interests are very much dependent upon America's ability to project its presence on the world's waterways. This is certainly one of the major missions of the U.S. Navy.

Ammunition Ship

USS Mount Hood, AE-29, replenishes ammunition of combat forces in forward area of operations.

Combat Stores Ship

USS San Jose, AFS-7, carries refrigerated stores, dry provisions, technical and aviation spares, general stores, fleet freight, mail, and other items. Uses two helicopters to transfer cargo to ships underway.

Fast Combat Support Ship

USS Sacramento, AOE-1, carries fuel, munitions, dry and refrigerated stores, and freight to ships underway.

Fleet Ocean Tug

USNS Powhatan, T-ATF-166, tows fleet ships damaged in battle or disabled for other reasons; conducts salvage operations, and supports other missions.

Replenishment Oiler

USNS Henry J. Kalser, T-AO-187, carries heavy loads of fuel, with some smaller cargo of dry and refrigerated stores, and some muntions. Capable of transferring fuel to receiving ship while both are underway. (The acronym for this procedure is "UNREP" -- underway replenishment.)

Aircraft

Aircraft are essential weapons in U.S. Navy and Marine Corps missions. The range, power, speed, and detection capabilities of the many military aircraft so profoundly enhance our ability to respond to any kind of threat that it would be unthinkable to plan defense without them. So specialized are their missions that the loss of even one category of aircraft from our arsenal would vastly inhibit the performance of the whole network of naval defense.

The following pages offer summaries of the missions and capabilities of most of the military aircraft seen in this area. These are not the only aircraft flown by the Navy and Marine Corps, by any means, but they typify most of what can be observed in San Diego skies.

Aircraft Identification Letters and Numbers

Military aircraft are designated by letters and numbers (AV-8B) as well as by name (Harrier). These letters and numbers have a special significance in describing the plane and its function. This identification system is simplified here for the lay person.

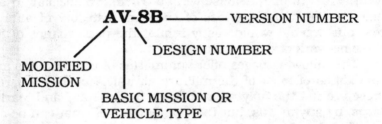

Look at the identification AV-8B, which refers to the Harrier Jump Jet. A letter to the immediate left of the hyphen tells vehicle type (G-glider, V-vertical take-off/landing, H-helicopter) or the plane's basic mission. In this case, the vehicle type is "V," or vertical take-off and landing. The "A" to the left of the "V" tells the modified mission of the plane, which is attack. To the right of the hyphen are a number and letter. The number tells which design this is, namely the eighth design of this general category of plane. The letter to the far right denotes the particular version of this design. The "B" version is the second version.

Helicopters are denoted by an "H" to the immediate left of the hyphen. The designation "SH-2G" is a helicopter (H) with a modified mission of anti-submarine warfare (S), second design, seventh version (2G).

Some of the letters included in aircraft identification are:

A-attack
B-bomber
C-transport
D-director
E-special electronics installation

F-fighter
H-helicopter (when used to denote vehicle type); search and rescue (when used to denote modified mission)
K-tanker
L-cold weather
M-multi-mission
O-observation
P-patrol
Q-drone
R-reconnaissance
S-anti-submarine
T-trainer
U-utility
X-research

Fighting Falcon

F-16N Fighting Falcon

The F-16 originated as an exploration into the question of whether it was possible to build a good fighter plane that was smaller and cheaper than the Air Force's F-15 Eagle. After the development of the F-16 prototype, however, the plane was so well-liked it was selected in late 1974 as an air combat fighter by both the United States Air Force and some European nations.

The U.S. Navy today uses the 14th version of this plane, the F-16N Fighting Falcon, as an adversary plane against which pilots train at the famed "Topgun" Naval Fighter Weapons Training School at Miramar Naval Air Station. The F-16N is useful in this regard, because it mirrors some of the characteristics of enemy fighter planes.

The Navy cannot use the F-16N for its fighter or attack missions off carriers. In carrier-based aircraft, the airframe, landing gear, and instrumentation must be built specially to withstand the terrific shock of take-offs and landings aboard an aircraft carrier. The F-16 was developed by the Air Force for land-based deployment, and therefore, is not constructed with the durability necessary for carrier use.

The Fighting Falcon has a long, sharp nose with a needle-like data probe on the end of it. It is a single-seat plane in which the pilot sits beneath the bubble canopy and flies by means of a sidestick controller. Set back along the plane's underbelly is an air intake, which, when viewed as part of the plane's complete profile, looks a bit like a shark's mouth.

The Fighting Falcon can carry missiles and is equipped with a built-in rapid-fire gun. But for training purposes, live fire — obviously — is not exchanged. Instead, the offensive and defensive movements and firing of both training pilot and adversary are recorded and analyzed electronically by ground computers and instructors.

Goshawk

T-45A Goshawk

There is no inexpensive way to train jet pilots. It is a costly enterprise involving the selection and preparation of pilots, support personnel, fuel, and the acquisition and maintenance of the aircraft. Yet there can be no substitute for thorough training — not in any American service — and certainly not in the Navy or Marine Corps, where pilots must land on aircraft carriers and amphibious assault carriers that must look no bigger than a raft when viewed from the height of a jet plane's final approach. Any money-saving training techniques, then, must offer better training for less cost.

That is the claim of the T-45A Goshawk, which denotes not only an airplane, but an entire training system that includes aircraft simulator, computer-based academic materials and instruction, plus practical flying experience in the Goshawk itself.

The Goshawk is a small, tandem-seat (room for pilot and student pilot), single-engine plane that can achieve a maximum speed of .85 Mach at 30,000 feet. It can operate from an aircraft carrier and has a range of 1,000 nautical miles. The Navy plans to acquire 300 Goshawk aircraft and 32 simulators. The T-45A training system and aircraft update training technology that has been in use for 30 years.

Greyhound

C-2A Greyhound

The C-2A Greyhound is the transport version that evolved from the E-2A Hawkeye radar plane. The Greyhound, like the Hawkeye, can be catapulted off, and can land on, aircraft carriers, which other transport planes that carry similar weights cannot do. Thus, the C-2A becomes essential in what the Navy calls COD or Carrier Onboard Delivery.

The cabin of the Greyhound can be transformed to accommodate such diverse cargoes as jet engines or litter patients being evacuated from combat areas. It can be loaded via a large aft cargo ramp/door and powered winch. The Greyhound's wings fold back for better utilization of carrier deck space and servicing.

The Greyhound is easily recognized by its two turboprop engines and four small vertical stabilizer fins set into its horizontal stabilizers.

Harrier

AV-8B Harrier

The AV-8B Harrier evolved from the famous British Harrier Jump Jet, so called because it can take off directly upward from a runway or carrier deck, using lift from a system that rotates the engine exhaust downward. The Harrier must diminish partially its payload either in weapons or fuel when it takes off this way. Yet, with a mere 100-yard-long take-off, it can lift its maximum gross weight of 29,750 pounds.

The U.S. Navy itself does not use the Harrier. It is flown by Marine Corps pilots, usually in training for support of amphibious assaults on hostile shores. The plane is used for light attack and close air support for ground forces, but it also can be used to defend the amphibious assault carrier on which it rides.

The Harrier uses air-to-ground ordnance to pinpoint attacks on enemy targets that may be quite close to the troops the plane is trying to protect. The Harrier can fire its weapons and reload either aboard the amphibious assault carrier or at makeshift landing sites close to the action.

The Harrier is a comparatively small jet, shorter in length by almost 20 feet, and shorter in wing span by about 34 feet than the F-14 Tomcat, for example. The Harrier flies at a maximum speed of 547 knots to a ceiling of 50,000 feet.

Hawkeye

E-2C Hawkeye

The E-2C Hawkeye probably has the most distinctive configuration of any naval aircraft. It is a fixed-wing propeller plane with a huge, round dish (24 ft. in diameter) mounted above its fuselage. This rotating dish is a radar dome containing complex electronic sensors that allow its crew to provide early warning of offensive movements, analyses of threats, and control of action against air and land targets.

While a two-person crew flies the plane, three other crew members monitor what is happening in the combat area below, forwarding radar, aircraft, and combat information to the battle commander aboardship. If the battle commander were to rely solely on shipboard sensing equipment, he would have a greatly reduced view from what is possible aboard a Hawkeye flying at a maximum ceiling of almost 31,000 feet.

About three-fourths of the total cost of this $46 million airplane is attributed to the onboard electronics systems. But such systems are indispensable in a combat setting in which technology reduces decision-making time to a matter of minutes or even seconds.

The Hawkeye is powered by two turboprop engines. It has a distinctive tail configuration. Instead of a large vertical stabilizer that would interfere with the sweep of its radar, it has four smaller vertical fins arrayed along its horizontal stabilizers.

Hercules

KC-130F Hercules

The Lockheed C-130 Hercules was a bold innovation in air transport when introduced in 1954. It had a pressurized fuselage with rear doors that could be fully opened in flight. These doors were situated in the portion of the plane where the underbelly takes a steep rise to meet the stabilizer fins, making the doors easily accessible for loading.

These aspects of the Hercules design, plus the adaptability of its roomy interior and the fact that its wings ride high on the fuselage, gave the aircraft the capability to accomplish several missions. In Vietnam, for example, it was used for the typical transport cargoes of men and materiel, but it was also equipped as a night gunship.

Today, more than 40 versions after its beginning, the C-130 Hercules is used by about 55 countries around the world. The U.S. Navy uses it for many tasks. It is a link in communications with ballistic missile submarines. It is used to refuel helicopters and other aircraft and to transport equipment and supplies. Sometimes it is equipped with skis to provide support for the scientific exploration of the Antarctic. The Hercules also launches and controls drone aircraft.

This plane has four turboprop engines that can lift a maximum load of about 175,000 pounds. The Hercules measures almost 100 feet long with a wingspan of 133 feet. While its exterior has retained its simple configuration, its interior has been adapted over the years to reflect improvements in avionics and other technology.

Hornet

F/A-18 Hornet

The F/A-18 Hornet, the nation's first strike-fighter, originated from what really was a funding problem. In the Fiscal Year 1975 Appropriations Bill, Congress forced the Navy to develop a fighter plane that could use the same basic design as that being developed for the Air Force's Lightweight Fighter Program. The object was to cut research and development costs, as well as production costs, for both services. It also represented an effort to come up with a fighter plane that could be used to some extent in lieu of the very expensive ($34 million) F-14 Tomcat.

The result was the F/A-18 Hornet, the letters F/A denoting its dual mission as a fighter and attack plane. It is a single-seat, fixed-wing plane, a much less sophisticated jet than the Tomcat and about 10,000 pounds lighter with a full payload. Nevertheless, the Hornet is a valuable design that gives the Navy and Marine Corps great flexibility and effectiveness in meeting a variety of commitments.

The Hornet can operate from either aircraft carriers or ground bases. It has a 20mm cannon built into it, but it carries missiles as its main weapons. In its role as a fighter, the Hornet travels light, with a maximum gross weight of 36,628 pounds at take-off, armed with Sparrow and Sidewinder air-to-air missiles. In its attack mission, the Hornet can take off with a maximum gross weight of 51,900 pounds, armed with both guided and conventional air-to-ground ordnance.

The Hornet can achieve a speed of more than Mach 1.7 and fly at a maximum of 50,000 feet. Pilots say the plane performs extremely well and requires a minimum of "down time."

Intruder *and* Prowler

A-6E Intruder

EA-6B Prowler

The A-6E Intruder is a carrier-based jet. It is a two-seat bomber that flies at subsonic speeds (up to 560 knots) and can deliver a pinpoint blow either to enemy ships or land-based targets. The Intruder's weight, when the plane is fully armed, is heavier than some of the four-engine heavy bombers of World War II. Yet it flies well even at slow speeds. A very rugged and sophisticated aircraft, it can do its job in complete darkness and in any weather.

The A-6E Intruder can be confused with its kin, the EA-6A/B Prowler, because both planes have basically the same airframe. In addition, they both have a bent refueling probe extending from the front base of the canopy up and out over the nose.

The Prowler, however, is a completely different plane with a completely different mission. It is designed to carry and operate complex electronic systems, including aircraft jamming devices and radar equipment. The Prowler is unarmed. It can be differentiated from the Intruder by the electronics pod on its vertical stabilizer fin and by the target-sensing pod under its nose.

Orion

P-3C Orion

The P-3C Orion is the Navy's front-line land-based aircraft for anti-submarine warfare. No other aircraft designed to hunt and kill submarines has the range or the payload capacity of the Orion. It has a mission radius of 2,390 nautical miles, and if it is to remain on station for three hours at 1,500 feet, its mission radius is 1,346 nautical miles. Its maximum gross take-off weight is 142,000 pounds, compared to about 67,000 pounds when empty.

The Orion carries a variety of highly sophisticated sensor equipment that enables it to detect, classify, track, and destroy enemy high-performance submarines. Detection, flight, navigation, and automatic firing capability all are supported by an onboard digital computer. The Orion carries anti-ship and anti-submarine weapons, as well as sonabuoys (floating sonar equipment).

The Navy wants to develop an anti-submarine aircraft with longer range and greater capability than the Orion, but until that time, the present fleet of Orions will be upgraded to meet the challenge of ever-increasing capabilities of enemy subs.

Osprey

The V-22A Osprey is intended to enter service in the near future. Named for the fish hawk that hunts along the shore lines of oceans, lakes, and rivers, the Osprey operates like both a helicopter and a plane. At the edges of its wings are two engines that can operate vertically or facing forward. This is why it is called a tiltrotor aircraft. When it takes off and lands, its propellers face the sky like helicopter rotors. Once it is airborne, the engine/transmission nacelles rotate 90 degrees forward, and the rotors become propellers.

All American military services will fly the Osprey, which will offer a distinct advantage with its tiltrotor capability, high speed, and combat ceiling of 22,200 feet. No helicopter can offer such advantages. The Marine Corps will fly the Osprey as a vertical assault transport for troops, equipment, and supplies, operating it from amphibious assault ships or shore bases. The Navy will use the Osprey for combat search and rescue, delivery and retrieval of special warfare teams, and fleet logistic support. The Osprey's rotor blades and wings fold for stowage aboard ship.

As of this printing no official photographs of the Osprey are available. Due to recent discussions in Congress over the budget-cutting process, the future of the Osprey is in question.

Skytrain

C-9B Skytrain

The C-9B Skytrain is a DC-9 Series commercial airliner used to airlift supplies and logistical material to combat areas. It also transports naval reservists to and from training sites. With a full payload, DC-9 airplanes built for the Navy have a range of almost 2,000 miles, the "longest legs" of any DC-9s ever built. In the passenger configuration, the C-9B Skytrain carries 65,283 pounds. In the cargo configuration, it carries 59,706 pounds.

Tomcat

F-14 Tomcat

The F-14 Tomcat, which caught the public fancy in the hit movie, "Top Gun," is the premier air defense fighter in the U.S. Navy, and perhaps, in the world. Capable of more than twice the speed of sound, the F-14 in its A+ through D versions, is powered by two turbofan engines with afterburners, developing up to 29,000 pounds of thrust per engine. It is scheduled to be fitted with even more powerful engines.

The F-14's specialty is the interception of enemy planes. It flies high (to a ceiling above 50,000 feet) to defend against attack before the enemy is within range or position to launch its missiles. The Tomcat's complex electronics and sensing equipment provide an incredible array of information, so much so that a navigator/radar operator (sometimes called "R.O." or "GIB" — Guy in Back) is needed to monitor the data while the pilot maneuvers the plane.

The navigator sits directly behind the pilot, informing him of the condition and location of his own and other planes, enemy movements and strikes, the location of the aircraft carrier, and many other important pieces of information. The Tomcat can track up to 24 targets simultaneously, attack six of them with its Phoenix air-to-air missiles, and still continue to scan the airspace.

The F-14 takes off with its wings spread to their full span of 64.1 feet, but they are swept back automatically as the plane gains speed. The plane is highly maneuverable in close-air combat and can fly day or night in all weather conditions. The Tomcat carries a variety of weapons in addition to Phoenix missiles, including Sparrow and Sidewinder missiles and a 20mm Vulcan cannon.

Viking

S-3 Viking

The S-3 Viking is a carrier-based aircraft that uses its sophisticated electronics and radar to hunt for enemy submarines and provide surveillance of surface shipping. The Viking is a subsonic plane with a range of 2,300 nautical miles without refueling. It can fly in any weather and is powered by two turbofan engines.

Through the use of sonabuoys and magnetic anomaly detection (MAD) equipment, the Viking can "see" even the new high-speed, deep-submergence, quiet submarines in addition to the older submarines that are easier to spot. In the event of open hostilities, the Viking also can destroy enemy subs and ships, using torpedoes, depth charges, missiles, rockets, and special weapons.

The Viking usually works from the middle to outer ranges of a carrier battle group, cooperating with other antisubmarine warfare units. It can work independently or with its partner, the land-based, long-range P-3C Orion.

3

Helicopters

Helicopters are an absolutely essential part of the Navy on land and sea. These aircraft have so many functions it isn't possible to list them all. Briefly though, helicopters are used to communicate, transport, track, lift, protect, hunt, and strike. Their mission dictates their range, speed, and configuration. The helicopters pictured on the following pages are identified by name and mission.

Seahawk

SH-60B Seahawk

The SH-60B/F Seahawk extends the sensors and weapons systems of surface ships for anti-submarine warfare, anti-ship surveillance, and targeting. It accomplishes this by deploying sonabuoys, processing magnetic anomaly detection information, and acting as an elevated radar platform, thus increasing the radar range of the ship. The Seahawk also carries two Mk-46 torpedoes to attack submarines.

Sea King

SH-3H Sea King

The SH-3H is the eighth version of the Sea King, which first was flown 20 years ago. It is a twin-engine, all-weather, ship-based, anti-submarine warfare helicopter. It is equipped with active and passive sonabuoys, magnetic anomaly detection equipment, data link, chaff, and a tactical navigation system. Replacement of the Sea King by the SH-60F Seahawk began in 1987.

Sea Knight

UH-46A Sea Knight

The UH-46 Sea Knight is a double-rotor helicopter that flew in its original version in 1962. Almost three decades later, this durable design, altered to take advantage of advanced power and technology, is still being flown. The Navy flies the UH/CH-46 for vertical replenishment, the Marine Corps flies the CH-46 for troop transport, and both fly the HH-46 for search and rescue.

Seasprite

SH-2F Seasprite

The SH-2G Seasprite is smaller and lighter than the Sea Hawk, but its job is similar. It is a ship-based anti-submarine warfare and anti-ship surveillance and targeting helicopter. It carries a search radar, electronic support measures, and magnetic anomaly detectors. It has an acoustic processor so it can conduct autonomous missions against submarines, and it can add such components as dipping sonar, missiles, or other weapons. The accompanying photo shows the SH-2F, a prior version of the Seasprite.

Sea Stallion

CH-53 Sea Stallion

RH-53D Sea Stallion

Like the CH/MH-53E helicopters, the Sea Stallions have two different letter designations to denote two different jobs. The CH-53A transports supplies and equipment. Its secondary mission is to transport personnel and evacuate troops. It can carry a payload of 37 troops or 24 litter patients plus four attendants. Maximum cargo is 8,000 pounds.

The RH-53D is basically the same as its counterpart, but with upgraded engines and special gear for its role as an aerial minesweeper.

Super Stallion

CH-53E Super Stallion

The CH-53E Super Stallion is a ship-based workhorse designed to carry cargo and troops internally, and oversized equipment externally. The Super Stallion has several missions, including the transfer of damaged aircraft, transport of containers, nuclear weapons, and equipment, and airborne mine countermeasures. It is the only helicopter strong enough to lift some of the new weapons systems used by the Marine Corps in their assault operations.

Sea Dragon

Along with its Super Stallion twin, the MH-53E Sea Dragon is the largest helicopter in the Western World, having a maximum gross weight of 73,500 pounds when fully laden. It is a multi-mission aircraft, but one of its jobs is that of minesweeper. Its external configuration is almost identical to that of the Super Stallion.

Facilities

The U.S. Navy and Marine Corps operate many facilities, both big and small, in San Diego County. We have provided summaries of some of the best-known military bases in this area, almost all of which are within the City of San Diego.

Marine Corps Base Camp Pendleton is not within our city limits. It is located about 45 miles north of San Diego. The quick glimpses of Marine Corps training visible from the I-5 freeway near Oceanside are enough to spark the interests of tourists who pass the base. That is why we have extended our range to include Camp Pendleton.

It is well to note that while many of the facilities listed in this section belong to the Navy, the Marine Corps also has a significant presence in San Diego City and County. Recruits are trained at the Marine Corps Recruit Depot (MCRD). Infantry and other personnel are trained at Camp Pendleton. Marines often participate in training with the Navy for such missions as amphibious assaults. Tourists visiting Navy ships will notice security is provided by Marines. Therefore, although the Marine Corps does not have the range of facilities in San Diego County that the Navy does, it is important to remember that the Marine Corps is officially part of the U.S. Navy; and socially, economically, and geographically, it is also part of San Diego.

Public Affairs Offices

U.S. Navy and Marine Corps installations in San Diego County are listed in the local phone book, with most Public Affairs Office (PAO) numbers and some addresses listed as well. We have included here some of the PAO numbers and addresses of the more widely known bases.

The public will find PAO staffs extremely busy, although helpful and polite. Here is a good rule of thumb for contacting them: If possible, send a letter specifying your tour or information requests. It's much easier for them to handle than a phone call to their besieged offices.

(For the following numbers, use Area Code 619.)

Commander Naval Base San Diego........................**532-1430**

Marine Corps Base Camp Pendleton......................**725-5566**
    Joint Public Affairs Office
    Building 1160
    Camp Pendleton, CA 92055-5001

Marine Corps Recruit Depot (MCRD).....................**524-1365**
    Public Affairs Office
    Marine Corps Recruit Depot
    San Diego, CA 92140

Naval Air Station Miramar.....................................**537-4082**
    Public Affairs Office
    Naval Air Station Miramar
    San Diego, CA 92145

Naval Air Station North Island
    Base Operator..**524-0444**
    Public Affairs Office.......................................**545-8167**
    (Do not call the Public Affairs number to arrange a visit
    aboard an aircraft carrier. For this tour, follow the
    instructions on Page 78.)
    Public Affairs Office
    NAS North Island
    San Diego, CA 92135-5100

Naval Submarine Base, San Diego
    Public Affairs Office
    Submarine Group Five
    158 Sylvester Road
    San Diego, CA 92106-3521
    Information available only upon written request; no
    telephone number available.

Naval Station San Diego (Foot of 32nd Street).....556-7354
    Public Affairs Office
    Code OI
    Box 16
    Naval Station San Diego
    San Diego, CA 92136
Naval Training Center..524-4210
    Public Affairs Office
    Naval Training Center
    San Diego, CA 92133-5000

Marine Corps Base Camp Joseph H. Pendleton

Traveling south from San Clemente or north from Oceanside is a journey with a scenic surprise. Between these two cities lies a 125,000-acre tract of land that is peaceful to the eye and a refuge to hundreds of species of plants and animals that might face extinction if their habitat were not encompassed within this mammoth preserve.

It is hard to believe this tranquil interruption of urban sprawl is Marine Corps Base Camp Joseph H. Pendleton, where thousands of recruits, active duty Marines, and Marine reservists are trained in amphibious and infantry warfare. When civilians employed on the base, as well as the Marines' families, are added, the total population of Camp Pendleton reaches about 50,000.

Traveling north on I-5, the tourist sees to the left the walls of the Landing Craft Air Cushion (LCAC) Facility, where the Navy works together with the Marines to perfect amphibious assault techniques. Near that facility, one also may see

Nearly camouflaged against the green hills of Camp Pendleton, Marines shoot live ammunition at targets. (Photo by Joni Halpern)

the huge CH-53E Super Stallion helicopters as their pilots practice landings and take-offs. To the right of the freeway are the barracks where recruits from MCRD spend a week aboard Pendleton for marksmanship training and testing.

The interior of Camp Pendleton may be toured only by car. The route begins at Oceanside and ends at Las Pulgas Gate, at I-5 south of San Clemente.

To start your tour, pull off I-5 at the Camp Pendleton off-ramp and stop at the Main Gate. To obtain a vehicle pass, a current driver's license, car registration, and proof of insurance are required. A booklet explaining the high points of Camp Pendleton's history and training facilities tells exactly which roads to take and where to stop. *Do not wander off the specified tour route.* Camp Pendleton conducts training exercises with live fire. Therefore, leaving the marked route can be dangerous! Also, the base is well-patrolled, and military police will issue tickets.

Within the tour, you may see three important aspects of Camp Pendleton. First, it is apparent the Marines take pride in their conservation efforts. They have biologists, game wardens, and firefighters to protect the land and its ecology. As a

Using his buddy as a stepping stone, a Marine scales a wall in Combat Town, while other Marines observe amid a touch of realism from smoke grenades. (Photo by Joni Halpern)

result, there are bison, coyotes, hawks, bald eagles, and many other wild creatures that roam the base.

Second, there are several historical sites that recall California's mission ancestry and subsequent rule by Mexico. The land now occupied by the base once was an important link between Missions San Luis Rey and San Juan Capistrano. Later, the land was owned by the Pico brothers, one of whom, Pio Pico, was the last governor of this area while it was under Mexican rule. The land was owned privately prior to its acquisition by the Marine Corps during World War II.

Beyond the sights that pertain to conservation or history, the visitor sees ample evidence of the seriousness of Camp Pendleton's mission — to prepare Marines for assaults on enemy shores, for infantry combat, and for the many support missions that sustain men in the field. Along the tour route, one may see tanks, artillery, amphibious vehicles, live fire ranges, and tiny "combat towns" where Marines learn to take control of enemy urban areas.

There is a great deal more going on at Camp Pendleton than that which is visible on the tour. Marines learn to use a wide variety of weapons and combat skills in both large and small groups in order to prepare themselves for any conceivable battle situation. Every Marine is considered a rifleman, so he must complete basic infantry training whether he works in an office or a mess hall. Camp Pendleton is the place where new Marines learn basic skills, specialists brush up on the basics, and experienced infantrymen and amphibious groups acquire advanced skills.

Camp Pendleton has 17 miles of beautiful shoreline, some of which is used for civilian surfing championships. The base leases land to the San Onofre Nuclear Generating Plant and to growers of tomatoes and flowers. There is housing and a 600-bed naval hospital aboard the base, as well as a host of facilities for Marine Corps personnel and their families.

For more information about Camp Pendleton, contact the Public Affairs Office listed on Page 66.

The object of Camp Pendleton training is to produce a skillful, resolute infantryman capable of confronting the enemy face to face.
(Photo by Joni Halpern)

Marine Corps Recruit Depot (MCRD)

A training unit of United States Marine Corps recruits stands at attention outside the mess hall at the Marine Corps Recruit Depot (MCRD) in Point Loma. Three drill instructors, their campaign hats pulled low over their eyes, growl out instructions in a drawl that is barely discernible to the uninitiated. It seems a recruit has licked his lips without permission and he's in big trouble.

"Get over here! Say 'Discipline, Sir,'" the sergeant orders.

"Discipline, Sir," says the recruit immediately, waiting to hear what punishment will follow.

To the civilian who glimpses this scene, there occurs the inevitable question: What could be so important about licking one's lips without permission that it must be punished?

The answer to that question lies on the battlefield, where an undisciplined movement can give away an entire unit's position or endanger the individual Marine or his comrades. The effort in Boot Camp is to simulate a battlefield mentality in which a man must be aware of every move he makes. He must exert an incredible amount of self-discipline over the smallest impulses. He must sacrifice his momentary personal needs or whims to the safety and success of the mission at hand.

There is no easy way to teach this. A Marine is not a Marine until he has weathered 11 weeks of some of the toughest training the American military has to offer. Today's Marines are there because they want to be. They endure long hours of physical training, marksmanship, combat skills, and military indoctrination. Their day starts at 5:30 a.m. and ends at 9:30 p.m. They are constantly under the critical eye of three drill instructors per training unit. Almost nothing about a recruit's appearance, performance, or behavior goes unnoticed.

The training is stressful for the drill instructors as well. They never ask their recruits to do what they cannot do themselves. They are absent from their families every third night to stay over with recruits. And many drill instructors will admit it takes a real effort to maintain the stressful pitch required to change a young man into a Marine.

On graduation day, held nearly every Friday of the year at MCRD, these young men are addressed as "Marines" for the first time. There is pride among them as they accept this name along with their entrance into the elite "Band of Brothers" that is the United States Marine Corps. MCRD graduates about 22,000 Marines each year.

To arrange a visit to MCRD or to attend a graduation ceremony — always open to the public — write or call the Public Affairs Office listed on Page 66. The public also may visit the Command Museum at MCRD, where early Marine weapons, aritifacts, and uniforms are on display.

On graduation day at MCRD, smiles and hugs symbolize new friendships formed during the ordeal of Boot Camp. (Photo by Jules Raabe)

Drill instructors are on the prowl during physical training. There is rarely a moment when recruits are not under the watchful eye of instructors. (Photo by Jules Raabe)

Recruits lift weights as part of a strenuous exercise program. By the end of Boot Camp, recruits are two to three times stronger than when they entered. (Photo by Jules Raabe)

Naval Air Station Miramar

Flying a jet plane is looked upon by many of us as the most glamorous job in the military. The jet pilot sits in a small cockpit just behind the plane's nose, with the wild blue visible through his bubble canopy and nothing but engine behind him. It must be a thrill to be at the controls of such a powerful machine.

But it is also dangerous. Most Navy jets are designed to operate off an aircraft carrier, a floating airbase with literally tons of offensive power delivered primarily by the pilots of the carrier air wing. From the moment these men take off, launched by powerful steam catapults, they are at risk.

The risk is abated as much as possible by a massive network of support provided by the Navy. One of the pillars of naval support and flight training is Naval Air Station (NAS) Miramar — Fightertown, U.S.A. — situated on 24,000 acres between I-15 and I-805 just south of Mira Mesa. The public knows it as the home of "Topgun," the naval fighter weapons and training school. But actually, that is only one small part of what goes on at the base.

NAS Miramar is like a city unto itself. Its personnel come from all over the country, so there are several types of housing on base, along with the social, medical, and recreational facilities to support the resident population.

But the working portion of NAS Miramar is involved in the monumental task of training pilots to fly the fighter jet and the airborne early warning plane, the E-2C Hawkeye. There are a host of support units that contribute to the job, including those devoted to aviation maintenance, aviation physiology training (covering such instruction as water survival, ejection training, etc.), naval oceanography (weather and aircraft routing), and aviation engineering. These units and others support the work of the many pilots who teach and train at NAS Miramar.

Because of security concerns, and because the equipment used in training is either bulky or dangerous, *the public is not permitted to tour this air station. Instead, NAS Miramar opens its doors to the public on a weekend each August for one of the greatest air shows in the world.* Last year, nearly half a million people witnessed the displays and live performances of almost

100 different aircraft, including those flown by the renowned Blue Angels' flying team.

For information about the air show, call or write NAS Miramar Public Affairs Office listed on Page 66.

In this practice procedure, a Navy pilot braces himself in the simulated single-seat cockpit of the Dilbert Dunker, just before plunging underwater. The pilot then must free himself and return to the surface. (Photo courtesy of the U.S. Navy)

The F-14 Tomcat, canopy up, looks a bit ungainly from the front. But in the air, it is sleek, fast, and deadly, one of the premier air defense fighters in the world. (Photo by Joni Halpern)

The different sized openings in the rear of this F-14 are caused by the tail feathers, which are constricted on the left and open on the right. Constricting the tail feathers increases thrust. Also visible here are the vertical stabilizers (reaching upward), the wings (parallel to the ground), and the horizontal stabilizers (slanted toward the ground). The wings sweep back automatically as the plane picks up speed. (Photo by Joni Halpern)

Naval Air Station North Island

North Island is a place of historical firsts. It is where Charles Lindbergh first embarked on the flight that would take him to New York for his transatlantic crossing to Paris. It is the place where the first naval aviator, Lt. Gene Ellyson, was trained in 1911. It was among the first airbases where the Navy was able to work closely with civilian manufacturers to develop and test ship-based aircraft.

Naval Air Station North Island was commissioned in 1917. At the time, the island really was separate from the rest of the Coronado land mass. But during the 1940s, the gap was closed by fill dredged from the harbor. Today, both physically, socially, and economically, NAS North Island is connected to the City of Coronado. Thousands of civilian and military personnel travel through Coronado on their way to work at the base. Many naval retirees live in Coronado. And the renowned Coronado Bridge, connecting the island to San Diego, almost surely wouldn't have been built if it hadn't been for the huge work force, now numbering almost 24,000, aboard NAS North Island.

NAS North Island is home to some naval commands which have broad responsibilities throughout the U.S. Pacific Fleet. The operations at NAS North Island comprise only one aspect of these commands. For example, while the office of Commander Naval Air Force, Pacific Fleet (COMNAVAIRPAC) is located at North Island, the scope of this command spans 100 million square miles of ocean in which the Pacific Fleet operates.

Three aircraft carriers — USS Ranger, USS Constellation, and USS Independence — are based at North Island. Often, one of these carriers will be open for tours at specified times during the year. *To participate in a tour*, phone the NAS North Island base operator at the number listed on Page 66. Ask which carrier might be available for tours. Then ask for the phone number of the Public Affairs Office aboard that carrier. This is where permission for tours originates. Ask for a reservation.

Once your participation in the tour is confirmed, your name will appear on a list which will be checked when you arrive at NAS North Island Main Gate. You will have to present a current driver's license, car registration, and proof of insurance to obtain a pass to drive your car to the parking lot nearest the carrier.

It should be noted that an aircraft carrier tour involves a fair amount of climbing on narrow ladders. Participants should wear comfortable shoes; slacks are suggested for women. Cameras are allowed, but your tour guide will advise as to what may be photographed.

NAS North Island covers 2,800 acres and is home base to 26 squadrons, including several helicopter squadrons. Six anti-submarine squadrons are based there as well, flying the electronically sophisticated twin turbofan jet, the S-3A Viking.

The Fleet Logistics Support Squadrons fly a variety of aircraft to support the Pacific Fleet's need for men and materiel. These aircraft range from the big Douglas C-9B Skytrain II to the light plane, Beechcraft UC-12B Super King Air. Both training and actual support missions are flown from NAS North Island using various logistics support aircraft.

NAS North Island has limited base housing, but it offers the full range of attendant services to support its military personnel.

For more information about the base, contact the Public Affairs Office listed on Page 66.

First stop for visitors to Naval Air Station North Island is the Main Gate pictured here. (Photo by Justin Halpern)

Two S-3 Vikings fly over Naval Air Station North Island. (Photo courtesy of U.S. Navy)

The island of an aircraft carrier rises to considerable height, as seen here on USS Independence, moored alongside the wharf at Naval Air Station North Island. (Photo by Justin Halpern)

Naval Station San Diego (Foot of 32nd Street)

There are many concerns that must be addressed when a ship returns home, including repairs that could not be made at sea, personnel matters, the medical, dental, and family matters of crew members, specialized training, and supply. These and other problems of men and materiel must be tended to while the ship is in port.

One of the largest naval installations providing this broad range of logistic and support services is Naval Station San Diego, a 733-acre base located at the foot of 32nd Street along South San Diego Bay. Naval Station San Diego is home to 87 surface ships and two component commands, the Navy Brig and the Transient Personnel Unit. The Navy Brig is a prison where sentences longer than one year can be served, although most sentences are much shorter. The Transient Personnel Unit keeps track of military personnel between duty stations.

Naval Station San Diego is a busy, working base. Group tours sometimes are arranged in advance, but there are no individual public tours. Normally, individuals or small groups are not permitted to tag along on group tours that have been pre-arranged.

There are many services that must be performed to keep ships and their crews in a constant state of readiness. Naval Station San Diego has 49 commands and activities to accomplish this. It offers fleet training, legal services, ship maintenance and repair, medical and dental clinics, family services, housing, shopping, recreation, and many other services.

Not all the activities under the jurisdiction of this base are located on the base itself. The Missile Test Center, for example, is located at Point Mugu, California, the Naval Weapons Station at Seal Beach, California, and the Naval Amphibious School here at NAS North Island.

For more information about Naval Station San Diego, contact the Public Affairs Office listed on Page 67.

The 3,000-ton, 438-foot frigate USS Bagley rests on a 12-foot-high cradle in a dry dock at Naval Station San Diego. Ship repair is only one of many services provided by the base for Navy ships homeported in San Diego. (Photo courtesy of U.S. Navy)

Naval Submarine Base, San Diego (Ballast Point)

Situated on a little finger of land jutting into the harbor from the Point Loma Peninsula is the site of San Diego's discovery by Spain. This is the place where Portuguese explorer Juan Rodriguez Cabrillo claimed the land for Spain in 1542 and named the peaceful harbor San Miguel Bay.

Years later, long after explorer Sebastian Vizcaino had renamed the bay as San Diego, Cabrillo's landing place became known as Ballast Point. History is not clear as to whether the Yankee traders gave it this name because they picked up its cobblestones as ballast or deposited them after taking on a cargo of cattle hides.

Today, Ballast Point is Naval Submarine Base, San Diego, a shore command that oversees and services 18 nuclear-powered fast attack submarines, one diesel submarine, two submarine tenders, and two floating dry docks. About 6,000 Navy and civilian personnel staff the base and ships. The base is small, so its facilities are limited strictly to what is needed to support, service, and train its submarine squadrons.

This base offers some group tours of submarines, with strict limitations as to what can be seen aboard the boat. The Public Affairs Office requires tour requests to be submitted in writing three weeks in advance. Only organized groups are allowed. This would include such groups as social, civic, or professional organizations (i.e. Boy Scouts, Rotary Club).

Minimum age limit for tour participants is 10 years old. Visitors should dress comfortably and wear soft-soled shoes. Women are advised to wear slacks, as the tour involves some climbing and descending, as well as maneuvering in tight spaces. (Civilians will emerge with a new respect for the endurance of the submarine sailor.)

For additional information about Naval Submarine Base, San Diego, or to arrange a tour, contact the base Public Affairs Office listed on Page 66.

Ballast Point, or Naval Submarine Base, San Diego, is the small finger of land jutting out from the Point Loma Peninsula. (Photo courtesy of U.S. Navy)

Naval Training Center, Recruit Training Command

Often, parents are heard to say when they attend the graduation of their son from naval recruit training, "He's not the same boy who left home. He's more mature and responsible. He knows how to get along with all kinds of people."

This process of change takes place at Naval Training Center, Recruit Training Command, in Point Loma. From that first recruit haircut, which sheers a young man right down to his essence, naval recruit training is designed to teach responsibility and teamwork.

In eight-and-a-half weeks of training, a recruit will march about 600 miles, not in long treks, but in close-order drill and virtually everywhere he goes with his recruit company. He learns the Navy way of doing things, which is prescribed both by tradition and by the practical considerations that are paramount aboard ship.

To help recruits learn shipboard procedures and basic seamanship skills, training is conducted aboard the stationary ship, USS Recruit, built on a foundation of concrete to roughly two-thirds the size of a guided-missile frigate.

Among other skills recruits are taught, water safety and survival are essential. About 15 per cent of new recruits cannot swim well enough to pass a basic survival test, due to fear of the water or to lack of early exposure to swimming. After special instruction in a concentrated course, all but a few are able to pass. The small number of recruits who fail do not remain in the Navy.

The fifth week of training is Service Week. Recruits lend a hand standing watch, doing office work, helping in the chow hall, and doing a variety of tasks that give them a feeling for what is involved in keeping a base or a ship running.

Graduation ceremonies for naval recruits are among the most colorful sights a tourist can attend. There are performances by the Recruit Training Command's Drum and Bugle Corps, Fifty State Flag Team, Color Guard, and Crack Rifle Drill Team, all comprised of recruits. The Recruit Training Command graduates about 27,000 recruits annually.

The public may attend graduation ceremonies with permission acquired by contacting the Naval Training Center Public Affairs Office listed on Page 67.

The uniform of a new recruit includes white leggings, worn only during recruit training, and later, for participation in such ceremonial units as color guard. (Photo by Joni Halpern)

Having removed their dungarees while in the water, naval recruits tie knots in each pant leg. Holding onto the waistband and snapping it against the water traps air in the dungarees, turning them into a crude, but functional, life preserver. (Photo by Joni Halpern)

Set on a concrete foundation, USS Recruit, commissioned in 1949, is used to train recruits in shipboard procedures. The ship is visible along Harbor Drive in Point Loma. (Photo by Joni Halpern)

One of many colorful sights at Naval Training Center's recruit graduation is the Fifty State Flag Team, composed entirely of recruits. (Photo courtesy of U.S. Navy)

Naval Training Center, Service School Command

A ship is like a small community, a battleship or an aircraft carrier like a small city. In either case, a ship requires a high degree of self-sufficiency. Therefore, the Navy trains its personnel in hundreds of specialties that are essential aboard ship.

One of the locations where this training takes place is Naval Training Center's Service School Command (SSC) in Point Loma, where newly graduated recruits and experienced sailors learn such jobs as aviation storekeeper, ship's serviceman, seaman apprentice, welding, air conditioning and refrigeration, machinery repair, metals testing, electronics and electricity, data processing, communications, and more.

Some specialties taught at SSC are unique to the Navy. Ship maintenance and repair requires well-trained hull technicians, pattern-makers, mold-makers, and others who staff the Navy's foundries and repair shops. SSC teaches these specialties.

Emphasis at SSC is on practical experience as well as classroom theory. In Mess Management School, for example, students learn what is needed to prepare balanced meals for hundreds and even thousands of sailors, but practical experience is gained by preparing meals for the hundreds of students who attend SSC daily. Advanced students produce beautifully decorated cakes and fine meals for some of the Navy's local celebrations.

SSC is noted for its intensity of content and the quality of its instructors. Each year, the school graduates about 33,000 students who are prepared to fill the jobs that keep the Fleet running.

Airman Apprentice training at SSC includes firefighting instruction with hands-on experience. (Photo courtesy of U.S. Navy)

Communications is one only of the areas of study taught at Naval Training Center's Service School Command. Here, a sailor studies to become a radioman. (Photo by Joni Halpern)

A Few Questions and Answers

What is a homeport?

A homeport is the port city and specific naval facility that serves as a ship's base. It is the place where the ship's squadrons, divisions, and battle group maintain their headquarters. A homeport also provides facilities where the ship can be serviced, supplied, maintained, and its crew can receive additional training. Generally, families of the ship's crew live in civilian or military housing in the homeport city.

What is meant by "class of ship?"

A ship's class originates when the mission of a specific category of ship (i.e., destroyers, cruisers) changes sufficiently to require a new design. Sometimes the hull must be changed; sometimes other structures must be altered to make way for new technology. It is the ship's mission, along with the technology necessary to accomplish that mission, that determines ship design. When a design problem becomes severe enough that it cannot be corrected in an existing ship, a new class is born.

What is the role of women in the United States Navy and Marine Corps?

Women serve ably in many areas of the military. They are doctors, technicians, skilled craftspersons, pilots, mechanics, journalists, and much more. At this writing, at least one woman has been named commander of a Navy ship.

However, by Congressional mandate, women may not serve in combat positions in the U.S. Military. Therefore, there are no women on combatant ships in the Navy or serving as part of Marine Corps combat forces.

What is USNS?

The letters USNS, designating, for example, the hospital ship USNS Mercy, refer to United States Naval Ship. USNS ships are not part of the regular U.S. Navy fleet, the ships of which are designated by USS, or United States Ship. USNS ships are part of the Military Sealift Command, a fleet of more than 100 ships which provide a worldwide transport capability for all United States military forces. The Military Sealift Command is headed by a vice admiral of the Navy, but the ships usually are skippered by a civilian master. The crew consists primarily of civilians in government service, although some U.S. Navy specialists may serve aboard.

San Diego Guide to Military Ships and Planes

For additional copies of this book, visit your local bookstore or contact the publisher.

For groups and organizations, a discount price is available.

Please send me _____ copies of San Diego Guide to Military Ships and Planes by Joni Halpern. I am enclosing $7.95 for each copy plus $1.00 for shipping and handling.

Total enclosed is $ _____.
(Send only check or money order)

Allow three weeks for delivery.

NAME_____

ADDRESS_____

CITY _____

STATE_____ ZIP _____

PHONE _____

Send to:
　　　　PS Features
　　　　P.O. Box 6751
　　　　San Diego, California
　　　　92106-6751

Author's Note

It would be rare if a federal budget were adopted without some controversy over the amount devoted to the military. That is because it is very expensive, even using the most efficient and far-sighted planning possible, to build and maintain what the American public has said repeatedly that it wants: a military presence that will ensure its rights to world resources, world commerce, and a democratic way of life.

Technology has made this military presence both possible and necessary. Militarily, we can do things today that we could not even fathom 20 years ago. But so can our enemies. The transfer of technological information, both open and secret, has locked us into what seems to be an irreversible commitment to stay on top. The American public has signified that it feels endangered in second place, and our military and political leaders have sought to ensure that the preparations of our men and machines will keep us competitive with the most advanced military forces in the world.

This is a difficult task, and even during these last few years, in which we have witnessed the largest peacetime military build-up in our history, we still do not enjoy unchallenged supremacy, or even, in some cases, parity, in every area of military strength. In all likelihood, the battle to achieve and maintain a competitive military edge will go on until the world learns better ways than the use of arms to solve its problems.

In addition to the built-in problem of this unavoidable escalation of technological development, the American military is faced with the task of preparing for more than one kind of war. It must arm itself to deter a long-range nuclear holocaust and at the same time, arm itself to wage conventional warfare with modern weapons. Finally, it must tailor its forces and weapons to achieve limited displays of power and protection within narrow, and often, politically motivated, parameters.

The wonder of the American military is that in spite of its might, it still relies on, and believes in, the ultimate direction of a civilian government. Certainly there are intense confrontations and backroom goings-on when military leaders are trying to save a preferred budget or program. But when the hand of Congress comes down with a clear directive against a military request, the military acquiesces. It is a restraint that honors only a very few governments in the world.

Military preparedness in a free country does not exist without public support. Its scope and duties are funded and directed by an underlying public sentiment, a feeling people have for how they want to be seen and treated in the world. Thus, the American public claims ownership of its military strength and readiness. The United States Navy and Marine Corps in San Diego provide a fascinating exhibit of the breadth of that ownership.

J. H.
1989

Glossary

Abaft — To the rear of. Use instead of "aft of."

Active-duty — Full-time service as distinct from inactive, retired, or reserve duty.

AEGIS — A modern, integrated, total combat system for combatant ships. It can take multiple aircraft and missile targets under fire simultaneously.

Aft — behind, rear.

Afterburner — Part of a jet engine into which fuel is injected and ignited by exhaust to increase thrust for short periods.

Airframe — Generic term including all parts of an airplane except the power plant, armament, and electronic gear.

Airspeed — Speed of aircraft through and relative to the air and distinct from groundspeed.

Air strike — Fighter attack aircraft assigned an offensive mission against specific objectives.

Air wing — The aircraft of an attack carrier, made up of squadrons.

Altitude — The height of an aircraft above a reference point. True altitude is height above sea level, corrected for temperature. Absolute altitude is height above ground.

Amidship(s) — In or toward the middle of a ship.

Amphibious — Capable of operating on land and sea.

Amphibious operation — Attack launched from the sea by naval and landing forces embarked in ships or craft.

Anti-submarine warfare — All-inclusive term embracing all techniques used against enemy submarines.

Armor — Steel or other protection against projectiles, in ships, aircraft, or special uniform.

Arresting cables — The cross-deck cables attached to the arresting engine and designed to engage the tailhook of an aircraft to bring it smoothly to a halt.

Astern — Toward the back or end of a ship or formation. Generally used in the sense of behind, or out of, a ship.

Battle group — An aircraft carrier, a battleship, if available, one or more AEGIS cruisers, a unit of destroyers, and a logistic support ship make up this typical offensive unit of the fleet.

Beam — Extreme width of a ship or a boat.

Bow — The front or forward part of a ship.

Bow door — Hinged or forward section of a landing craft or ship over which cargo is unloaded when craft is beached.

Bridge — Ship's superstructure, topside and usually forward, that contains control and visual communication stations.

Brig — A prison for military personnel.

Brow — Portable bridge or ramp between the ship and a wharf, pier, or dock.

Buoy — Floating object, anchored to the bottom, that indicates a position on the water, an obstruction, or a shallow area, or that provides a mooring for a ship.

Carrier Onboard Delivery — System of delivering support items and mail from shore to aircraft carrier that is underway.

Catamaran — A boat or a ship with two parallel hulls.

Catapult — A device, powered by steam, for launching aircraft from a ship's deck at flying speed.

Chaff — Any of several types of metallic reflectors used to confuse enemy radar.

Combatant ship — A ship whose mission is to engage in warfare with the enemy.

Deploy — Generally, to send ships or squadrons abroad for duty; specifically, to change from a cruising or approach formation to a formation of ships for battle or amphibious assault.

Depth charges — Anti-submarine explosives dropped from ships.

Derrick — A device consisting of boom and tackle, used for hoisting heavy objects.

Docking well — A basin built into a ship at its stern that allows seawater to enter to a level sufficent to float landing craft for launch and recovery.

Electronic warfare system — A generic term for anything from a particular radar system, range finder, to a bomb launch computer, or other device that updates older analog systems.

Elevator platforms — Large platforms on aircraft carriers or assault carriers used to lift aircraft from the hangar deck to the flight deck.

Fantail — The aftermost deck area topside in a ship.

Flagship — The ship from which an admiral or other unit commander exercises command.

Flight deck — Top deck of an aircraft carrier or assault carrier.

Forward — Toward the bow.

Funnel — Ship's smokestack; stack.

Galley — A shipboard kitchen.

Guidon — Company identification pennant for Navy or Marine Corps units ashore.

Hatch — Water-tight cover over deck opening in ship or submarine.

Hull — The body or shell of a ship or seaplane.

Island — Structure above the flight deck of an aircraft carrier containing command and flag bridges, the primary flight control station, radars, anti-aircraft weapons, and much more.

Jamming — Involves the use of techniques and electronic devices to render ineffective enemy radar and detection.

Knot — A measurement of speed equivalent to one nautical mile per hour (6,076 feet per hour).

LAMPS — Light Airborne Multi-Purpose System. A helicopter with all its support equipment, including landing platform and the ship carrying it.

Mach number — The ratio of an object's speed to the speed of sound. An aircraft traveling at Mach 1 could be moving at about 758 mph, depending upon the temperature and density of the air.

MAD — Magnetic Anomaly Detector. A device that allows low-flying aircraft to detect a submerged submarine by making use of the magnetic field of the submarine's submerged mass.

Mine countermeasures — Procedures for preventing or reducing damage to ships from mines. Includes channel conditioning, clearance, disposal, hunting, loading, sweeping, watching, and any other measure found necessary as a result of increasingly sophisticated mine warfare.

Mission radius — The distance designed into the capability of any ship, boat, or aircraft that includes reaching its destination and returning to its point of launch or deployment.

Nautical mile — Length of one minute of the arc of the great circle of the earth, 6,076 feet compared to 5,280 feet of a statute mile.

Quarters — Living spaces aboard a ship.

Radar — Radio detection and ranging; an instrument for determining, by radio echoes, the presence of objects and their range, bearing, and elevation.

Range — Distance to target.

Salvage — To save or rescue material that has been discarded, wrecked, sunk, or damaged.

Saturation diving — A type of deep-sea diving in which a diver's body tissues are allowed to absorb their full capacity of inert gases, permitting the diver to stay below longer and surface faster than would be possible under ordinary diving conditions.

Screen — Ships stationed around such a unit as a battleship or aircraft carrier to protect it.

Ship's company — Everyone assigned to a ship, but distinct from the air crew.

Silent (pertaining to submarines) — Condition of quiet operation of machinery in a submarine to deny detection by an enemy listening for noise.

Sonabuoys — Floating sonar devices, both active and passive, laid in the water to detect passing ships or submarines.

Sonar — Underwater detection achieved by analyzing sound. Active sonar emits sound and analyzes its reflection. Passive sonar merely listens. When active sonar emits a sound, it gives away its own location; passive sonar avoids this danger. Dipping sonar is equipment that can be trailed through the water by helicopters or hydrofoils.

Stabilizers — Fixed horizontal and vertical fins that keep an aircraft stable as it moves through the air.

Superstructure — All structures above the main deck of a ship.

Underway Replenishment Group — A group comprised of fleet oilers, supply, and ammunition ships, along with their protective screen.

The great majority of definitions in this glossary are reprinted from: The Naval Terms Dictionary, 5th edition by Captain John V. Noel, Jr., USN (Ret.) and Captain Edward L. Beech, USN (Ret.). Copyright © 1988, U.S. Naval Institute, Annapolis, Maryland.